NATURE, CULTURE, AND INEQUALITY

NATURE, CULTURE, AND INEQUALITY

A Comparative and Historical Perspective

THOMAS PIKETTY

Translated from the French
by Willard Wood

OTHER PRESS
New York

Originally published in French as *Nature, culture et inégalités: Une perspective comparative et historique* in 2023 by Société d'ethnologie, Nanterre, France.
Copyright © Société d'ethnologie, 2023
English translation copyright © Willard Wood, 2024

This text is based on a talk given at the Musée du Quai Branly—Jacques Chirac on March 18, 2022, at the invitation of the Société d'ethnologie.

Production editor: Yvonne E. Cárdenas
Text designer: Patrice Sheridan
This book was set in Chaparral Pro
by Alpha Design & Composition of Pittsfield, NH

1 3 5 7 9 10 8 6 4 2

Library of Congress Cataloging-in-Publication Data
Names: Piketty, Thomas, 1971- author. | Wood, Willard, translator.
Title: Nature, culture, and inequality : a comparative and historical perspective / Thomas Piketty ; translated from the French by Willard Wood.
Other titles: Nature, culture et inégalités. English
Description: New York : Other Press, [2024] | "Originally published in French as Nature, culture et inégalités: Une perspective comparative et historique in 2023 by Société d'ethnologie, Nanterre, France"— Title page verso. | Includes bibliographical references.
Identifiers: LCCN 2024002605 (print) | LCCN 2024002606 (ebook) | ISBN 9781635424560 (hardcover) | ISBN 9781635424577 (ebook)
Subjects: LCSH: Equality—Cross-cultural studies. | Equality—History. | Social stratification—Cross-cultural studies. | Social stratification— History. | Capitalism—Moral and ethical aspects. | Capitalism— Environmental aspects.
Classification: LCC HM821 .P552313 2023 (print) | LCC HM821 (ebook) | DDC 305—dc23/eng/20240220
LC record available at https://lccn.loc.gov/2024002605
LC ebook record available at https://lccn.loc.gov/2024002606

CONTENTS

LIST OF FIGURES

NATURE, CULTURE, AND INEQUALITY

ARE THERE NATURALLY OCCURRING INEQUALITIES? THE LONG MARCH TOWARD EQUALITY

Inegalitarian systems—that is, the structure and degree of socioeconomic inequality in different societies, and their evolution over time—are extraordinarily diverse. We can make sense of the phenomenon only if we take into account the central role of history and human culture. Inequality has, in fact, followed markedly different trajectories— political, socioeconomic, cultural, civilizational, and religious. It is culture in the broadest sense—and, more particularly, collective political mobilization— that provides an explanation for the diversity, degree, and structure of the social inequalities we observe. In contrast, the importance of so-called natural factors (personal talents, reserves of natural resources, and other factors of this kind) is relatively limited.

Sweden, considered one of the most egalitarian countries in the world, provides an instructive example here. Some have attributed its egalitarianism to the country's ingrained characteristics, to a culture that has a "natural taste" for equality. In fact, Sweden was long one of the most stratified countries in Europe, highly sophisticated in the political organization of its inequality. This situation changed very rapidly in the second third of the twentieth century, in response to a concerted social and political effort, after the Social Democratic Party came to power in the early 1930s. This party, which then governed continuously for the next half century, put Sweden's governmental capacities toward an entirely different political program than had existed before.

Sweden thus provides an interesting case, one that should inoculate us against any belief in long-term determinism, according to which certain natural or even cultural factors might make some societies forever egalitarian while making others (India, for example) forever inegalitarian. Social and political forms can change, sometimes much more quickly than contemporary observers think. Those who benefit most from a system tend, for obvious reasons, to see inequalities as part of the natural order, and they are apt to characterize disparities as permanent and inevitable, warning against any change that might threaten the existing harmony. In fact, reality is highly changeable and always being rebuilt: it is the product of power relations, institutional compromises, and partially explored forks in the road.

But looking beyond this great diversity of inegalitarian systems, we can recognize a basic movement over the course of the past centuries: a tendency toward greater social equality. This trend started at a particular point in history and not, for instance, in Neolithic times or in the Middle Ages. It is part of the historical development that had its origins in 1789—call it the end of the eighteenth century—and it has led toward increasing political and socioeconomic equality.

Limited in extent, this gradual movement toward equality has been a halting, chaotic process in which social conflict has played an extremely important role. And it has called for various forms of collective learning. In my book *Capital and Ideology* (2019; English translation 2020), I laid out the theme of collective learning about just institutions, specifically around the question of borders: What are the outlines of the community one belongs to? How are political power and the political system organized within this community? The same goes for property: What are the collective rules that define the limits and extent of property rights? What do you have the right to own? What does it mean to be an owner?

These two central questions—borders and property—are thus sources of conflict and directional change, with each country trying to learn from its own trajectory and all too often forgetting the trajectories of other countries. Each country follows its apprenticeship trajectory, which in the long term tends toward greater equality, even if the motion is hesitant and punctuated by retrograde phases.

Finally, overarching the diversity of inegalitarian systems and the limited trend toward equality, there exists another type of relationship between nature, culture, and inequality that I'd like to examine here and that I'll address in the last part of this text: global warming, CO_2 emissions, and the destruction of nature and biodiversity. This issue will occupy an ever-more-central place in the decades ahead. It may lead to a greater demand for equality than we've recently seen: there can be no resolution to the global warming crisis, no possible reconciliation between man and nature, without a drastic reduction in inequality and without a new economic system that is radically different from the current capitalist one. In describing this system, I refer to "a participatory, democratic, and ecological socialism," but other terms could clearly be devised—and no doubt will be. At all events, I consider it imperative to reopen the discussion on changing the economic system and reimagining its long-term development.

THE EVOLUTION OF INEQUALITY
AND INEGALITARIAN SYSTEMS

The elements I intend to present here come in part from my book *A Brief History of Equality*, first published in France in 2021, and in part from the World Inequality Database (which issued the *World Inequality Report 2022*). This database on global inequality is the product of a collective effort and draws on the work of more than a hundred international researchers. Under its aegis, historical data has been collected that allows us to track changes in the distribution of income and wealth over long periods—sometimes more than three centuries.

The field of social and economic inequality itself has a long history, and I've simply followed on earlier efforts. Among my predecessors are Fernand Braudel, Ernest Labrousse, Adeline Daumard, François Simiand, Christian Baudelot, Gilles Postel-Vinay, and many others. There is a great tradition in France, starting in the early twentieth century, of historians, sociologists, and economists engaging in the task of collecting data on salaries, income, profits, plots of land, and inheritances. I had the good fortune to start working at a time when the digitization of this data made gathering knowledge much easier. In fact, what's striking when one rereads the works of Labrousse or Daumard is that the labor of collecting data was done by hand, often at the expense of anything else. Inheritance data had to be culled from archives in Paris and the provinces, where it was stored on file cards. This involved considerable work but left little in its wake that could be used by later researchers. The resulting studies, labeled "serial" history, have all but disappeared from view, partly because the organization and description of the data collection itself took up such a large part of the researcher's energy, to the detriment of historical analysis. Today, obviously, the task of data collection is much simpler and is performed on a comparatively vaster scale, in a directly cumulative context.

Furthermore, the fact of explicitly integrating the twentieth century into the long timeframe studied (which was not the case with the first wave of

serial historians, who mainly dealt with the eighteenth and nineteenth centuries) necessarily puts
history, and especially politics, at the very center of
the analysis. When you consider the eighteenth century, or even the nineteenth, you can easily be led
to believe—wrongly, I would say—in fateful trends
that operate independently of political developments. But with the twentieth century, the connec-
tions jump out at you the moment you draw a curve
showing salaries, income, and wealth: World War I,
World War II, the liberation of France, the events of
May 1968, et cetera. You immediately have to factor
in political history to explain the inflection points
you're seeing. I want to emphasize right away that
I'm talking about the constructive and collective
aspects of political history. Contrary to what some
have claimed, equality has not been the product of
wars per se, nor of great catastrophic events such
as the Black Death. In the case of the French Revolution, war even tended to stifle revolutionary developments. And World Wars I and II had relatively
little effect on equality in many countries: it all de-
pended on the societal structures and outcomes that
were implemented afterward. Political mobilization
and union pressure were more important in bringing about a shift, for instance, in Sweden, where the

two world wars had relatively little impact. In the United States, it was largely the economic crisis of the 1930s and not World War I that led to instituting social welfare policies. The real force for change derives, as we'll see, from concerted social and political pressure, as well as the ability to build new institutional outcomes.

I had the good fortune, as I mentioned, to start my career as a researcher in this intellectual context, along with an international network of researchers like those who have contributed to the World Inequality Database. It allowed me to enlarge my comparative and historical focus and to observe the great diversity of inegalitarian systems and the halting progress toward equality that I spoke of earlier. So as to give a preliminary sense of the diversity of systems of inequality around the world, I'll start by presenting results relating to a very simple criterion: income distribution. Afterward, I'll go on to look at the distribution of wealth. Let's quickly define the difference between these two terms: income is what is earned in the course of a year, either as remuneration for one's work or from one's wealth (in the form of rent, interest, dividends, et cetera); wealth is what one owns (housing, business assets, securities, et cetera), and it is always distributed much more unequally than income. The possession of capital also determines the structure of power relations: this is obviously true for the ownership of business assets and the means of production, and it is also true for the possession of housing and the framework for reproducing private and family life, as well as the ownership of the state and public power through public debt, which can take different forms.

INEQUALITY OF INCOME

Let's start, then, with income. We use a fairly simple metric for this: the share of total income going to the top 10 percent of earners. By definition, in a perfectly egalitarian society that share would equal 10 percent of total income, since those earners represent 10 percent of the population. In a perfectly inegalitarian society, they would take all the income, a share of 100 percent. What actually happens, of course, lies somewhere between the two extremes. As shown in figure 1, the share going to the top 10 percent is lowest in Northern Europe (20 to 30 percent), and highest in South Africa, where that share reaches 70 percent. This should give you a first glimpse of the considerable variation in levels of inequality across the globe.

If you were to try, looking down from a great height, to decide which were the most egalitarian

FIG. 1 Share of income going to the top 10 percent globally, 2022

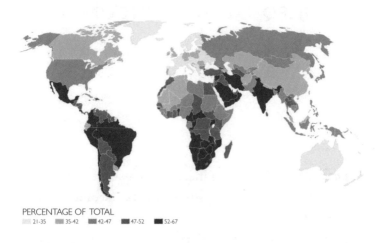

PERCENTAGE OF TOTAL
21-35   35-42   42-47   47-52   52-67

FIG. 2 Share of income going to the bottom 50 percent globally, 2022

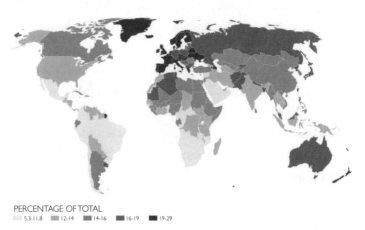

PERCENTAGE OF TOTAL
5.3-11.8   12-14   14-16   16-19   19-29

and inegalitarian parts of the world, the first thing you'd notice is a great deal of variation, sometimes even within a single region: in Latin America, for instance, Argentina is more egalitarian than Brazil or Chile, in keeping with the country's sociopolitical history and the groundwork laid by Juan Perón to build a welfare state, which was realized more fully there than in any of the neighboring countries. But some regions do show a higher degree of overall inequality: South Africa, with its legacy of apartheid, and southern Africa generally; and Latin America as a whole has a high degree of inequality of property, tied to Spanish colonization and the political regimes that followed; North America, for its part, bears traces of specific racial inequalities. Generally speaking, colonial legacies have left a strong and lasting mark on the structures of inequality. But there are also areas, like the Middle East, where the sharp disparities are not due to a past history of racial or colonial inequality but to a modern fact, namely oil revenues, which have turned into financial revenues, concentrated among an extremely small share of the population. In the current map of inequality, we therefore see a mix of old and new, with different interlocking rationales.

Our metric for income inequality gives even starker results when we look at the lower end of the economic spectrum: What share of the total national income goes to the poorest 50 percent (fig. 2)? There again, you have to keep proportionality in mind. In a perfectly egalitarian society, the poorest 50 percent would receive 50 percent of total income. Conversely, in a totally inegalitarian society, they would receive nothing at all. In fact, the number stands at 5 or 6 percent of total income in the most inegalitarian countries (South Africa, for instance), and 20 or 25 percent in the most egalitarian (again, Northern Europe). Nowhere does it reach 50 percent. When we say that this portion of the population receives 25 percent of total income, it means that the average income of the poorest 50 percent is approximately half the national average. This certainly reflects a fair degree of inequality, but less than where the bottom 50 percent are getting 5 percent of total income, meaning that the average income of the poorest group is a tenth of the average national income.

It's important in general to keep in mind the great diversity of situations. If we take stock only of a country's gross national product (GNP) or its average national income, we may completely overlook very real factors that affect the living conditions of sizable groups within that society, since in two countries with the same average income, the share distributed among the poorest 50 percent may vary by a factor of from one to five according to the income distribution model (it's roughly 5 percent of total income in South Africa and roughly 25 percent in Sweden). Consequently, when we look at how poverty develops, we miss a great deal if we look only at average income as a whole.

It would be impossible to account for this variation in inequality on the basis of "natural" factors. The disparities cannot be attributed to differences in personal talent, native endowment, or natural temperament—and it would be very surprising for these talents to be distributed so unevenly between countries. Nor can we attribute the disparities to the countries' natural resources—there is oil in the Middle East and oil in Norway, yet their income distribution is entirely different. All the evidence suggests that it's the institutions chosen by these different societies, which are themselves the product of different social, cultural, political, and ideological histories, that lead to the wide disparity in levels of inequality.

INEQUALITY OF WEALTH

What we've observed for the distribution of income also applies to the distribution of wealth, with one important difference: wealth—meaning property, real estate, and business or financial assets—is always much more concentrated in a small segment of the population than revenue. In the case of revenue, the share going to the richest 10 percent varies from 25 to 70 percent, depending on whether we're looking at Sweden or South Africa. In the case of wealth, the share of the richest 10 percent is between 60 and 90 percent no matter where we look. At the other end of the spectrum, the poorest 50 percent, who received from 5 to 25 percent of income, do not own more than 5 percent of total wealth in any country on earth (fig. 3).

Basically, the poorest 50 percent never own anything, or just about. In Europe, and specifically

FIG. 3 The extreme concentration of capital—global wealth inequality by region, 2021

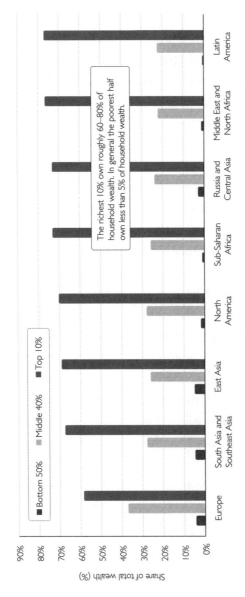

In Latin America, the richest 10 percent own 77 percent of household wealth, while the poorest 50 percent own just 1 percent. Net household wealth equals the sum of all financial assets (e.g., stocks and bonds) and nonfinancial assets (e.g., housing stock and land) owned by individuals, minus any debts. See: wir2022.wid.world/methodology.

in France, they own only 4 percent of total wealth. That is certainly better than in Latin America, where the figure is only 2 percent, but it is still a very low number considering that it is divided between half the population.

It's important to keep these figures in mind. When drawing up a global picture of inequality, we Europeans tend to rhapsodize (the French particularly) over how egalitarian our countries are. These figures help us keep things in perspective. Yes, there has historically been a stronger movement toward equality in France and Europe than in other parts of the world, but first, it didn't happen by itself—the movement was the result of hard-fought social and political battles; and second, it mainly affects the distribution of income, which has certainly been equalized somewhat in the past century. When it comes to the distribution of wealth, however, things have changed very little. In France a century ago, the share owned by the poorest 50 percent was 2 percent, the same as in Latin America today. It has risen to 4 percent today, which is certainly an improvement, but a trivial one that doesn't change the basic reality: property as a whole (financial, business, and real estate) is concentrated among an extreme few. If we look only at business capital, at the means of production, the picture is even more extreme. The share of the top 10 percent stands at 80 to 90 percent or more, and the share of the bottom 50 percent at practically zero. The welfare state itself has always been marked by an extreme concentration of economic power. The "great redistribution" of property that occurred largely between 1914 and 1980 has had a significant impact on reducing the disparity between the richest 10 percent and the next 40 percent, but it has had practically no effect on the bottom 50 percent.

GENDER INEQUALITY

In developing our methods and sources at the World Inequality Database, we generally aim as much as possible at compiling data that is comparable across different parts of the world. We first looked at income inequality, then wealth inequality; we subsequently developed a fairly simple metric for gender inequality: women's share of total income from work (salaries and income from unsalaried activity). If there were perfect equality, that number should be 50 percent. In actual fact, if you look at studies of the time spent working, which of course includes household work, women always account for more than 50 percent of hours worked. Ideally, their share of total income should therefore be more than 50 percent as well. What we see in practice, however, is that their share falls far below that number (fig. 4). And while there has been some

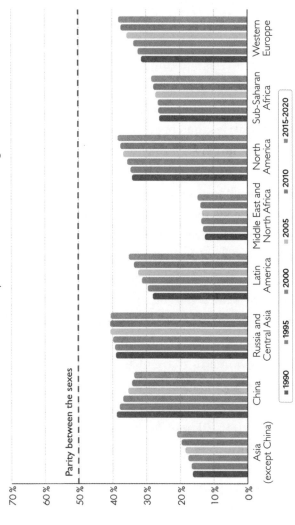

FIG. 4 Share of income from work received by women in different regions of the world, 1990–2020

From 1990 to 2020, the share of income from work that went to women in North America rose from 34 percent to 38 percent. See: wir2022.wid.world/methodology; and Theresa Neef and Anne-Sophie Robilliard, "Half the Sky? The Female Labor Income Share in a Global Perspective," World Inequality Lab—Working Paper No. 2021/22, December 2021.

progress (in Europe, for example, women's share of income has increased from 30 to 36 percent in the past few decades, still leaving 64 percent for men), there are countries moving in the opposite direction: China, whose communist legacy originally left women a slightly higher share of total income than in other countries, has been trending lower in recent decades, largely because of the huge increase in very high earnings, which mostly go to men, in China as elsewhere.

The metric we use has the advantage of giving a more accurate picture of the vast economic disparity between men and women than some others, which tend to sugarcoat reality: too often, we look simply at the salary gap for a given position, when the problem is that men and women actually don't have access to the same positions. What we measure here is women's share of total income. Obviously, this brings together many different factors: the pay disparity for any given position, which is on the order of 10 to 20 percent, but also the disparity between the kinds of jobs men and women can attain, the amount of part-time work they receive, the dearth of women in better-paying jobs, the low rate of promotions for women, et cetera.

In France, approximately 35 percent of total income currently goes to women and 65 percent to men. To put things in perspective, the share that went to women in 1970 was 20 percent, which is close to the level women receive today in India, South Asia, and the Middle East. In 1970, women were almost totally excluded from the monetary system and had very little buying power. There has definitely been progress in this area, though we shouldn't exaggerate its extent. The patriarchal economy is intimately bound to the development of capitalism, and our emergence from this system is still in its early stages, though it's striking once again to see how great the variations are between different countries and parts of the world, and how closely tied they are to different sociopolitical and historical processes.

AN UNEVEN MARCH TOWARD EQUALITY IN EUROPE

I'd like to return to the question of the historical development of inequality. France is one of the countries for which we have the most reliable historical data on income and, more particularly, on wealth and property ownership. This is owing to the system for recording inheritances and estates established at the time of the French Revolution, which has resulted in inheritance archives with unusually rich data going back to the late eighteenth century (fig. 5 and 6).

Thus, when it comes to income, we do see a movement toward greater equality in the last two centuries, especially in the twentieth. The share of income going to the richest 10 percent declined from 50 percent to 30 or 35 percent, while the share going to the poorest 50 percent rose from

10 or 15 percent to 20 or 25 percent. Yet the size of this change should be kept in perspective. The share going to the poorest 50 percent, as we've seen, is still well below the share going to the richest 10 percent, even though the poorest 50 percent are by definition five times as numerous.

The level of inequality is much greater when we look at the distribution of property, and the movement toward equality there is much more limited. We do observe a significant reduction in the share of total property belonging to the richest 10 percent, which drops from 80 or 90 percent on the eve of World War I to 50 or 60 percent today, but that share has started to rise again since the 1980s. So while it's important to recognize the long-term drop, we shouldn't exaggerate its size. Furthermore, this reduction has basically benefited the next 40 percent, those falling between the richest 10 percent and the poorest 50 percent. But the poorest 50 percent have hardly benefited from the redistribution of property in the past two centuries at all.

In Western Europe (Germany, the United Kingdom, France, and Sweden), the overall trends have been quite similar: between 1913 and 1920, there was a shift toward a slightly less extreme concentration of wealth (fig. 7 and 8). The novel development was the

FIG. 5 Distribution of income in France, 1800–2020: The start of a long-term movement toward equality?

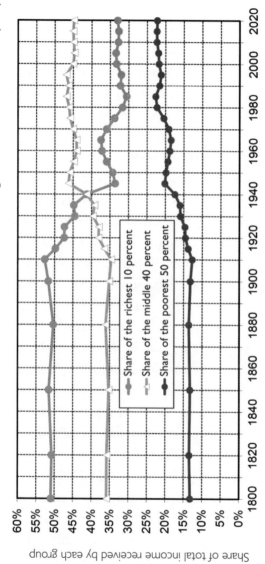

The share of total income going to the top 10 percent of earners, including income from work (salaries and wages, income from nonsalaried activities, retirement pensions, unemployment compensation) and income from capital (profits, dividends, interest, rent, capital gains, etc.) stood at around 50 percent from 1800 to 1910. After the two world wars, the income gap lessened, benefiting both the working class (the poorest 50 percent) and the middle class (the middle 40 percent), to the detriment of the upper class (the richest 10 percent). See: piketty.pse.ens.fr/egalite

FIG. 6 The distribution of property in France, 1780–2020: The gradual emergence of a propertied middle class

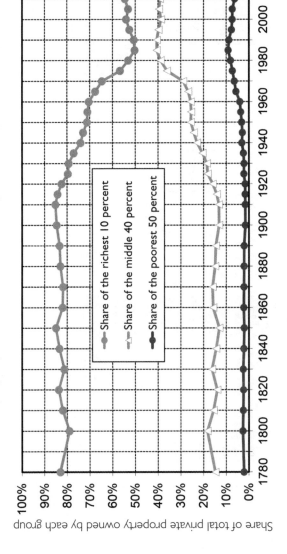

The share of total private property going to the richest 10 percent (including real estate, business assets, and financial assets, net of debt) hovered at 80 to 90 percent in France from 1780 to 1910. Property ownership became more widespread in the wake of World War I, a trend that stopped in the early 1980s and primarily benefited the "propertied middle class," defined here as the group between the disadvantaged classes (the poorest 50 percent) and the well to do (the richest 10 percent). See: piketty.pse.ens.fr/egalite

FIG. 7 The persistence of highly concentrated property ownership

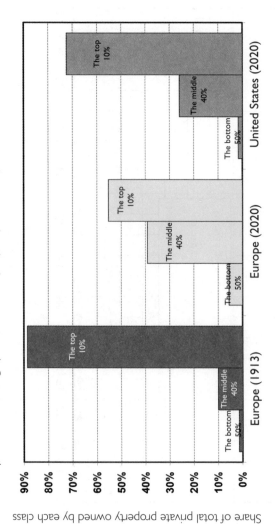

The share of total private property owned by the richest 10 percent in Europe in 1913 (averaged for France, the United Kingdom, and Sweden) came to 89 percent (with the poorest 50 percent owning just 1 percent); 56 percent in Europe in 2020 (with the poorest 50 percent owning 6 percent); and 72 percent in the United States in 2020 (with the poorest 50 percent owning 2 percent). See: piketty.pse.ens.fr/egalite

FIG. 8 Extreme inequality of wealth: European property-owner societies in the Belle Epoque (1880–1914)

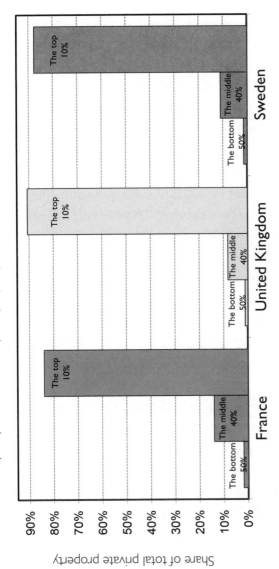

The share going to the wealthiest 10 percent (counting real estate, business assets, and financial assets, minus any debt) averaged 84 percent in France from 1880 to 1914 (as against 14 percent to the middle 40 percent, and 2 percent to the poorest 50 percent); 91 percent in the United Kingdom (as against 8 percent and 1 percent); and 88 percent in Sweden (as against 11 percent and 1 percent). See: piketty.pse.ens.fr/egalite emergence of what I have called the *property-owning middle class*. These 40 percent, who are neither the richest 10 percent nor the poorest 50 percent, owned practically nothing until 1913 and were thus almost as poor as the poorest 50 percent. There had been no middle class. Today, this group owns 40 percent of the total wealth of Western Europe and represents 40 percent of the total population: its average wealth is on the order of 200,000 euros per adult. The median in these households is 100,000 euros per adult, but the households may possess 100,000, 200,000, 300,000, or 400,000 euros. These are people who are not enormously wealthy but who are far from being truly poor and who resent being treated as such. The emergence of this group is a considerable event—economically, socially, and politically—even if access to wealth remains practically nil for the poorest 50 percent.

In Europe, the main characteristics are a persistent high concentration of property and the emergence of a property-owning middle class. What we see in the United States today is intermediate between the present state in Europe and its situation before World War I. The propertied middle class in the United States is shrinking, and whereas it once reached the European levels of 30 to 40 years ago, it is starting to drop closer to Europe's pre–World War I levels.

In a general way, the history of inequality in the countries of Europe before World War I is full of useful instruction. The period was a very rich one in comparison with the present period, and it has had a profound effect on my trajectory as a researcher. My friends and colleagues Gilles Postel-Vinay and Jean-Laurent Rosenthal and I were able to show that the degree of property concentration in France differed little from its concentration in the United Kingdom. This is significant, because political speeches made during the French Third Republic constantly contrasted France and the United Kingdom. A major theme of France's centrist elites—whether in politics, finance, or the republican movement—was the contention that "We are utterly different from the United Kingdom. Owing to the French Revolution, we are an egalitarian nation, and therefore we don't have to create progressive income or inheritance taxes. That's all very useful for a country as monarchical and highly inegalitarian as the United Kingdom, or as authoritarian as Prussia, but we French, who invented liberty and equality, are already a country of small landowners and have divided up our landed estates." Certainly, except that property had not been divided much at all in the first place, and in the second, landed estates no longer had much significance in 1913. While it was true that land ownership was more concentrated in the United Kingdom, this was secondary to the fact that, with respect to industrial capital or financial portfolios, which were invested all over the world at that time, it made little difference to the accumulation and concentration of fortunes whether you were a republic or a monarchy. France and the United Kingdom had similarly high levels of concentrated wealth. I was thus able, a century after the fact, to reveal the hypocrisy of a good many of that era's political speeches, including those of contemporary economists like Paul Leroy-Baulieu, who loudly insisted that France was a nation of small landowners.

The data, in fact, was starting to be put to use even at the time, because the inheritance tax had become slightly progressive in the wake of a 1901 law. This serves to show that a change in the institutional and fiscal system can free up information and make available a type of knowledge that can then be put to good use. For example, Joseph Caillaux was able to address the Chamber of Deputies and, using statistics on inheritance to support his claim, declare that France was not in fact a country of small landowners. The data was also used to create a tax on income in 1914, though its effect was muted given the new challenges the country then faced. France was practically the last Western country to enact an income tax. The majorities in the Senate and Chamber of Deputies that passed the law of July 15, 1914, did so not to invest in education but to finance the war against Germany. It was the one factor that could break the logjam, at a time when a progressive income tax had long existed in many Northern European countries, as well as in Japan, the United Kingdom, and the United States. That France was slow to sign on was partly due to its complacent belief in its own egalitarianism, based on the fact of the French Revolution.

THE EXAMPLE OF SWEDEN

I'd like to spend a little time now on another interesting case: Sweden, which is today generally considered an extremely egalitarian country. Yet this was not how things stood at the beginning of the twentieth century. All the countries in Europe were extremely inegalitarian, with Sweden intermediate on the spectrum between France and the United Kingdom. But in Sweden's case, the inequality had a very specific structure. With France and the United Kingdom, their colonial empires played a large role: colonial assets, holdings that resided in other parts of the world, were important parts of very large fortunes. This was much less the case in Sweden, obviously, where other factors relating to the political system were the primary contributors to a high degree of inequality.

From 1865 to 1910, Sweden had a particularly sophisticated system for qualifying voters on the basis of property ownership and tax status. Property-qualified voting persisted right up till World War I, whereas other countries, including the United Kingdom, had expanded voting rights during the nineteenth century. In Sweden, only the richest 20 percent of men could vote. Yet the system was even more restrictive, because an elector from those richest 20 percent might be entitled to anywhere from one to a hundred votes, according to his degree of wealth. The richer you were, the greater voice you had. Better yet, while there was a ceiling of one hundred votes for general elections, there was no ceiling at all for municipal elections! Consequently, Sweden had several dozen townships where a single voter cast more than 50 percent of the vote, making him a dictator with total democratic legitimacy. The country's prime minister, in fact, was almost always an aristocrat with more than 50 percent of the votes in his district.

Corporations and legal entities also had the right to vote in local elections until World War I, in proportion to the amount of capital they invested in a community and their income level. This is a privilege that today's multinational corporations would very much like to have. They sometimes find a way to achieve a similar result, but the fact they don't quite dare ask for it signals that an important change has occurred.

That Sweden retained a political system of this kind right up till World War I shows the inventiveness that human societies employ—and their dominant groups specifically—to structure the system of rights so as to preserve their own power. But it also illustrates the absence of any national or cultural determinism when it comes to inequality levels, because the country would soon be utterly transformed.

At the start of the twentieth century, Sweden was whipsawed between its political system, which privileged property ownership, and a working class that for a range of historical and religious reasons was highly literate compared to the working classes of other European countries. The Swedish labor unions and the young Social Democratic Party played on the strong general conviction that property owners had pushed their advantage too far and a new balance needed to be struck. A powerful tide of social and political pressure brought about universal suffrage in 1920. The Social Democratic Party was subsequently elected to power in 1932 and stayed at the helm almost continuously until the 1990s.

Since then, things have gotten more compli-
cated, and Sweden is much less in the forefront in
its tax policy, partly because of the international
community's refusal to join in real cooperation, and
the country is also much less in the forefront on
moving beyond capitalism. But from 1930 to 1980,
the Social Democrats put the state's resources toward a political program that differed radically
from what had gone before. They used the records
that had made it possible to measure income and
property not to allocate the right to vote according
to wealth but to impose a progressive tax, with the
goal of funding access to education and healthcare.
The measures that the Social Democrats enacted,
while not perfect, were a far cry from those of earlier periods. It brought about a level of equality
greater than anything seen elsewhere, and it happened in the space of a few decades, more or less
peacefully, but in response to a strong groundswell
of social and political pressure.

Sweden's example is interesting, because it
shows that a country is never inegalitarian or
egalitarian by nature. Everything depends on who
controls the government and to what end. The historical trajectory we see here undercuts any and all
determinism.

THE RISE OF THE WELFARE STATE: EDUCATION SPENDING AS AN EXAMPLE

In Europe, one of the most important factors for understanding the trend toward equality in the twentieth century is the rise of the welfare state. Here again, while the circumstances in different countries varied, the development was quite widely shared throughout Western Europe (the United Kingdom, France, Germany, and Sweden). Until World War I, the state's total levy on national income was less than 10 percent, which it used mostly to maintain order, enforce property rights, pay the police force and courts, and develop capacity for foreign intervention, in keeping with colonial expansion. Expenses other than those used to assert the state's authority were kept to a minimum. After

1918, a movement began that would lead to taxation on a much larger scale, and over the last thirty years, tax receipts for the four European nations mentioned above have remained stable at around 45 percent of national income (fig. 9).

Let's look at education, which is undoubtedly one of the most important factors in bringing about equality. Over the past century, public spending on education has increased tenfold, measured as a percentage of national income. Before World War I, it represented less than 0.5 percent of national income: the system was extremely stratified, and only a small minority could continue their education past primary school. Yet even primary school was poorly funded compared to secondary school and university. Today, the average spending for education in our four Western European countries comes to 6 percent of national income.

This increase in education spending has been a factor in promoting individual freedom, equality, and prosperity, reducing levels of inequality, and raising productivity and living standards. We are so used to government funding for education that we sometimes forget that this substantial development played a central role in the limited but real progress toward equality that I mentioned earlier.

FIG. 9 The rise of the welfare state in Europe, 1870–2020

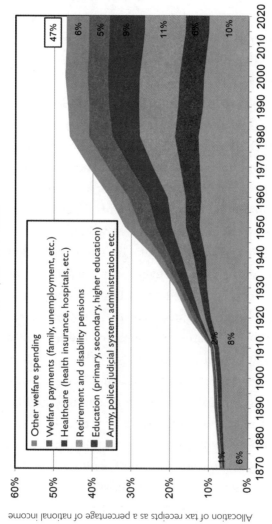

In 2020, the average total tax levy in Western Europe amounted to 47 percent of national income and was spent as follows: 10 percent of national income on state expenditures (army, police, judicial system, general administration, roads and other basic infrastructure, etc.); 6 percent on education; 11 percent on pensions; 9 percent on healthcare; 5 percent on social welfare benefits (excluding pensions); 6 percent on other welfare costs (housing, etc.). Before 1914, virtually all the money provided by taxation went to state expenditures. Source: See piketty.pse.ens.fr/egalite

But to qualify this statement somewhat, we should note that education spending has stagnated since the 1980s and 1990s, quite paradoxically, since access to higher education has increased during this period: while barely 20 percent of any age cohort went on to higher education in the 1980s, that figure has climbed to 60 percent today. In concrete terms, it means that the investment per student has declined. We've unfortunately seen this drop in per-student investment in France during the last fifteen years, especially in the least well-endowed fields of university study.

This phenomenon—fairly paradoxical in nature and running counter to the developments of the past century—is rooted in a system of political beliefs that since the 1980s and 1990s has maintained that the overall level of public spending and taxation must absolutely be held steady with respect to national income. Given that the share going to healthcare and retirement benefits has been increasing—not enough to keep pace with the public's needs, but increasing nonetheless—other spending has had to be reduced, and that's what has happened with education over the long run. Expanding the size of the welfare state could remedy these contradictions, but it would call for new milestones in tax justice and progressive taxation, on both a national and an international level.

And while there has certainly been progress toward a more equal distribution of the public investment in education, we shouldn't paint an idealized picture. Let's look at the inequality of investment in education in France (fig. 10). This data applies to the generation that is completing its education today, young men and women who turned twenty in the year 2020. In the graph, all those born in 2000 are ranked according to the total education spending they've received from kindergarten through advanced degrees. Briefly, those who receive the most public funds for education—on the order of 250,000 to 300,000 euros each over the course of their educational career—are those who follow long and well-financed courses of study—typically preparatory programs that prepare students for the competitive-entry higher institutions known in France as the *grandes écoles*, and the *grandes écoles* themselves. Those represented on the graph at the lowest levels are the young men and women who left school at sixteen or seventeen: they received funding only for primary and secondary education. And those in the middle are the students who followed a

FIG. 10 The inequality of education investment in France

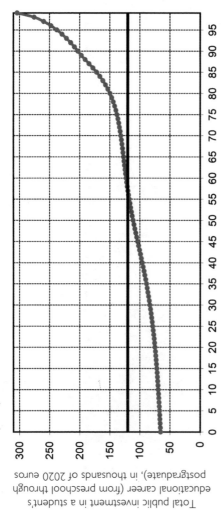

Total public investment in a student's educational career (from preschool through postgraduate), in thousands of 2020 euros

Ranking by percentile according to degree of investment in a student's educational career

On average, students reaching age twenty in 2020 received (from preschool to postgraduate degree) 120,000 euros in public spending (approximately fifteen years of schooling, at an average cost of 8,000 euros per year). The 10 percent of students in this generation who benefited from the least public investment received 65,000–70,000 euros, while the 10 percent who benefited from the greatest investment received 200,000–300,000 euros. NB: the average cost per year in the French system from 2015–20 varied from 5,000–6,000 euros for preschool and primary education, 8,000–10,000 euros for secondary education, 9,000–10,000 euros for university, and 15,000–16,000 euros for the preparatory course for entry to the *grandes écoles*. See: piketty.pse.ens.fr/egalite

FIG. 11 Colonies for the colonizers: Inequalities in education spending in historical perspective

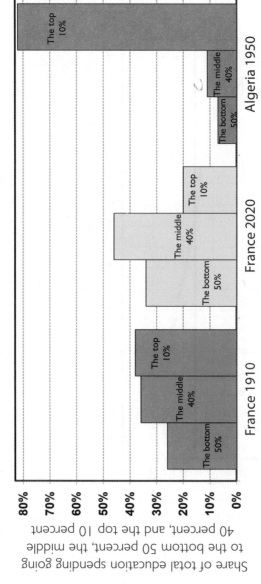

In Algeria in 1950, the 10 percent of students benefiting from the most public spending on primary, secondary, and higher education received 82 percent of total education funds. In comparison, the share going to the 10 percent benefiting most in France in 1910 was 38 percent, and, in France in 2020, 20 percent (which is still twice as high as their share of student numbers). See: piketty.pse.ens.fr/egalite poorly financed course of study at a university, such as a degree in humanities.

The individuals on whom the least was spent received 60,000 to 70,000 euros in education funds, while those on whom the most was spent received 250,000 or 300,000 euros, and those in the middle about 100,000 euros. Briefly, we see a disparity in public spending of 200,000 euros between those who received the least and those who received the most. Unfortunately, those who receive the most tend to come from a more privileged social setting than the others. Public spending therefore reinforces existing inequalities in quite a substantial way. This 200,000-euro differential is about the size of the average inheritance: it's as if the most privileged classes receive an additional average inheritance, this one a gift to them from the public coffers.

In the long run, access to education has actually expanded, but with two important qualifications: the inequalities are still substantial, and spending is at a much lower level than even in the recent past. I always come back to this paradox: our societies are still extremely inegalitarian, yet thanks to political battles and historical developments, they have made progress toward greater equality. What I have shown about the distribution of income and wealth also applies to the distribution of education spending (fig. 11). Today, the 10 percent of a given age group who receive the most public funds for education receive just 20 percent of total education spending. It is still a very large number, because the bottom 50 percent receive only about 35 percent. If the curve seems egalitarian, it is actually extraordinarily inegalitarian, since the 10 percent who get the most funding will get only 1.5 times less than the bottom 50 percent, although the latter are five times more numerous: briefly, the per-person spending for the top 10 percent is three times higher.

While the situation may seem more egalitarian today than in 1910, it is only because the system back then was even more stratified than it is now. For most social classes other than the well-heeled bourgeoisie, education ended after primary school. The bourgeois classes, on the other hand, had access to a system of higher education where a university professor's salary was many times that of a schoolteacher. The stratification of the education system led to much greater inequality than today, and the disparities were more marked.

In colonial societies, education was stratified to an even greater degree. Briefly, the top 10 percent, to take Algeria in the 1950s, were the children of the colonists, who accounted for a little more than 10 percent of the population. The rest, meaning the "Algerian Muslims," as they were then called, made up 90 percent of the population. The system was completely segregated, just as it was in the southern United States until the 1960s, where there were separate schools for whites and Blacks. In Algeria, there were schools for the children of colonists and schools for the children of Algerian Muslims. If you examine the budgets of that period—I draw here on the excellent research on the history of colonial budgets by Denis Cogneau, one of my colleagues at the School for Advanced Studies in the Social Sciences (EHESS)—it turns out that 80 percent of the total education budget went to the children of colonists, though they were only 10 percent of the population. Additionally, this spending drew on indirect taxes that fell mainly on the colonized. To reiterate, the colonial government was levying taxes on the whole population, the great majority of whom were colonized subjects, to finance a system that primarily benefited the colonists' children.

Our current educational system, then, whether we compare it to the colonial era or to France in 1910, is more open and more egalitarian. But the long-term trend toward equality has not reached its end point. We could well set other, different goals for the distribution of our investment in education, instead of speechifying about it in abstract terms. Constructing a norm for social justice also requires constructing tools that will allow citizens to deliberate and assess what's being done. When it comes to tax justice, for example, we have put a lot of time into developing a system that, with its notions of income, capital, tax rate, and tax schedule, allows us in theory to check up on the underlying norm of tax fairness. In the case of national education, we have a multicriteria system that doesn't really allow us to check on what's being done and in practice leads to the kinds of results I've described. Much could be improved.

MAKING RIGHTS MORE EQUAL

For my part, I am trying to develop an approach based on an equal right of access to fundamental goods: education, healthcare, and participation in politics. I have mentioned the example of the right to vote in Sweden, but it obviously doesn't end with equal suffrage: when it comes to funding for political campaigns and the media, we can imagine more egalitarian systems. I'm also very much thinking about all that pertains to economic democracy, that is, equal participation in the decision-making within businesses. I've taken an interest in the system of codetermination or shared management that we see in Germany and Northern Europe, where up to 50 percent of the vote is allotted to representatives of the salaried workers. This is not enough, because when voting is evenly split, the shareholders always get the deciding vote, but all the same it means that if a group owns 10 or 20 percent of the capital, it can tip decisions in its favor, even when a shareholder owning 80 or 90 percent of the capital stands in opposition. This is a significant development, one that arose in Germany and Sweden in the wake of World War II. Shareholders in France, Britain, or the United States would heartily dislike this system.

Yet it would be possible to push things even further. I support the idea, for instance, that of the 50 percent of votes assigned to shareholders, no single shareholder could control more than 10 percent. Such a system would come closer to providing equality of power, while preserving the possibility, in very small businesses, that a person who had brought a certain amount of capital toward a personal project might wield a slightly larger share of votes than someone who hadn't provided any capital but might be trying to get his or her own personal project approved.

This is the kind of thinking I'm trying to develop on the subject of equality in the face of economic clout. It doesn't call for a complete equality of results, because people have diverse aspirations: individuals will develop different plans, and absolute equality doesn't exist, neither when it comes to people's professions nor their incomes. What level of income disparity would be reasonable, given the difference in individual outlooks and choices of activity, and what level might be necessary as an incentive for social and economic organization? Income ratios of from one to three, or from one to five, might be compatible with these goals. But ratios of one to fifty are certainly not justified, as any number of historical experiments have shown.

The orders of magnitude I mentioned strike me as representing acceptable levels of inequality, but it is clearly a question that a democratic process and public deliberation should decide. Yet that would call for an equal ability to influence the political scene, and we are a long way from that.

PROGRESSIVE TAXATION

—◆—

I'd like to end by dwelling at some length on two further points that have to do with inequality: the question of progressive taxation on the one hand, and of the destruction of nature on the other.

The whole question of progressive taxation is extremely important. In the first place, it has been a topic of discussion for a long time. The chart below illustrates examples of two ideas discussed in France in the eighteenth century: one comes from Joseph-Louis Graslin, a town planner and economist from Nantes, while the other is from Sieur Lacoste, a more anonymous citizen. Both published pamphlets, of which a great number were produced during the revolutionary era: Graslin proposed a progressive tax on income, while Lacoste proposed a progressive tax on inheritance, calling it a "national right to inherit." These models, which were

TABLE I Proposals for a progressive tax in France in the eighteenth century

Graslin*: progressive tax on income		Lacoste**: progressive tax on inheritance	
multiple of average income	effective tax rate	multiple of average estate	effective tax rate
0.5	5 %	0.3	6 %
20	15 %	8	14 %
200	50 %	500	40 %
1 300	75 %	1 500	67 %

*Essai analytique sur la richesse et l'impôt, 1767. **Du droit national d'hérédité, 1792.

In the plan for a progressive income tax proposed by Graslin in 1767, the effective tax rate rises gradually from 5 percent for an annual income of 150 livres tournois (about half the average adult income at the time) to 75 percent for an income of 400,000 livres tournois (about 1,300 times the average income). A similarly progressive schedule for taxing inheritance was proposed by Lacoste in 1792. See: piketty.pse.ens.fr/egalite

not adopted at the time, have many points in common with the systems that a number of countries put in place in the twentieth century. Conceptually, it seems simple enough: the tax rate starts at 5 or 6 percent for incomes or estates falling below the general average but rises to 60, 70, or 80 percent once you reach incomes and estates worth 100 to 1,000 times the average.

A system of progressive taxation was instituted in late 1792 and early 1793 to pay for the wars, but the experiment was halted fairly soon, and the tax regime adopted at the end of the French Revolution is an absolutely proportional, or fixed-rate, system of taxation. Similarly, inheritances were taxed in a strictly proportional way: all during the nineteenth century, property transfers from parent to child were taxed at 0.5 percent, whether the value was one thousand francs or one million. There was no attempt at redistribution.

In 1901, the inheritance tax became progressive, with a tax of 2.5 percent for the top bracket. The rate would subsequently increase to 5 or 6 percent, specifically to fund the retirement law of 1910. Still, no dramatic shift toward progressive taxation really occurred until World War I (fig. 12 and 13). The highest income tax rate in France, applicable to the highest income earners, was 0 percent until 1914, since France had no income tax at all until the war. During World War I, things moved very fast, especially in the United States in the late 1910s. The process there was complex, as it required the passage of a constitutional amendment, but a strong groundswell of support for a just tax system existed in the United States at that time. Americans were determined not to become as inegalitarian, oligarchic, and plutocratic as old Europe, which was considered exceedingly inegalitarian. The general thought, shared even by relatively conservative economists, was that if the United States fell into the pitfall of becoming as inegalitarian as Europe, it would completely destroy the democratic system.

Starting in the late nineteenth and early twentieth century, therefore, the issue was one of great concern in the United States, and after income tax was allowed by the passage of the Sixteenth Amendment in 1913, it came to be used on an impressive scale. The phenomenon began in the early 1920s and received new impetus with Franklin Roosevelt's election in 1932. For the half century from 1932 to 1980, the income tax for the highest earners in the United States averaged 80 percent, climbing as high as 91 percent under Franklin Roosevelt. And these were just the federal income tax rates; there might be an additional state tax of 5, 10, or 15 percent.

Not only did this not squelch capitalism in the United States—we'd see the effect after a half century—but those years correspond to the period of the United States' greatest prosperity and its most complete economic domination of the rest of the world. Why? For the simple reason that income disparities of one to fifty or one to one hundred don't do much good. I don't say that we should

FIG. 12 The invention of progressive taxation: The top tax rates on income, 1900–2020

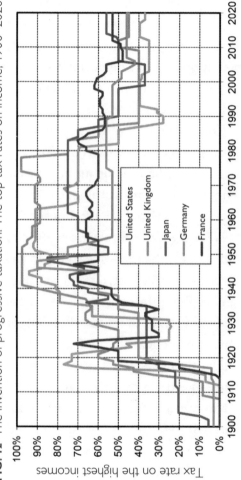

The tax rate for the highest incomes in the United States averaged 23 percent from 1900 to 1932, 81 percent from 1932 to 1980, and 39 percent from 1980 to 2020. For these same periods, the highest rate in the United Kingdom was 30 percent, 89 percent, and 46 percent; in Japan, 26 percent, 68 percent, and 53 percent; in Germany, 18 percent, 58 percent, and 50 percent; and in France 23 percent, 60 percent, and 57 percent. Taxes were most progressive in the mid-twentieth century, particularly in the United States and the United Kingdom. See: piketty.pse.ens.fr/egalite

FIG. 13 The invention of progressive taxation: The top tax rates on inheritance, 1900–2020

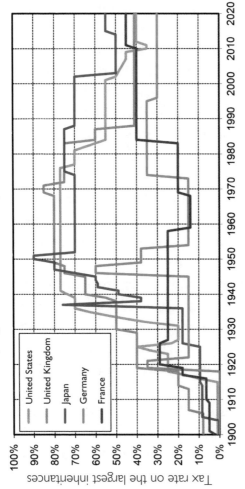

The tax rate applied to the largest inheritances in the United States averaged 12 percent from 1900 to 1932, 75 percent from 1932 to 1980, and 50 percent from 1980 to 2020. For these same periods, the highest rate in the United Kingdom was 25 percent, 72 percent, and 46 percent; in Japan, 9 percent, 64 percent, and 63 percent; in Germany, 8 percent, 23 percent, and 32 percent; and in France, 15 percent, 22 percent, and 39 percent. Taxes were most progressive in the mid-twentieth century, particularly in the United States and the United Kingdom.
See: piketty.pse.ens.fr/egalite

strive for complete equality; it may be that we should aim for a differential of one to five, or one to ten—judging from the database available to me, I'd think a disparity of one to five would work fine. But when you compare the different societies for which we have data, nothing justifies a ratio of one to fifty or one to a hundred. In the United States, a forceful reduction of this disparity through progressive taxation stifled neither economic growth nor innovation (fig. 14).

The factor that actually leads to greater prosperity is education. Until the mid-twentieth century, the United States enjoyed a considerable lead in education over the other Western countries. In the 1950s, 90 percent of a given age group in the United States received a high school education, in contrast to 20 percent in Germany, France, and Japan. These countries would not achieve such near-universal access to secondary education until the 1980s and 1990s. The lead that the United States enjoyed in productivity, especially in the industrial sector, derived from its lead in education.

In the 1980s, starting with Ronald Reagan's presidency, the country adopted a different paradigm. Reagan pointed to the failure of the Vietnam War, Carter's defeat at the hands of the Iranians,

FIG. 14 Effective tax rates and progressiveness of taxes in the United States, 1910–2020

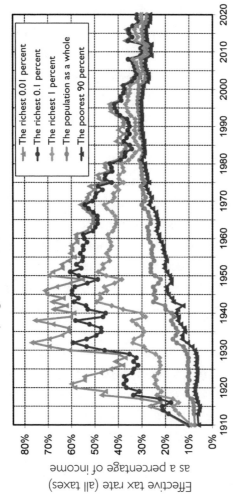

From 1915 to 1980, the tax system in the United States was highly progressive, in the sense that the effective tax rates on the highest incomes (adding all taxes together, and as a percentage of total pretax income) was significantly higher than the average effective rate paid by the population as a whole (and particularly the bottom 90 percent of incomes). Since 1980, the tax system has been only mildly progressive, with no more than minor differences between effective tax rates. See: piketty.pse.ens.fr/egalite et cetera, to reconsider Roosevelt's policies. He suggested that the country had gone too far and become almost communist; American entrepreneurship had to be revived by cutting the top tax rates, which dropped to 28 percent. That was the Tax Reform Act of 1986, which is the very definition of Reaganomics. Never again would taxes rise to their previous high levels.

This radical alteration to the tax system was meant to boost growth: in actuality, the growth of the U.S. economy in the period from 1990 to 2020 fell to half what it had been from 1950 to 1990. All the evidence suggests that the Reagan plan didn't work, but we are stuck today in the same political and ideological moment—of course, the system for financing political parties and the media has had a role to play in this.

The history of progressive taxation in the twentieth century is therefore a very rich one. Progressive taxes played a big part in making the general increase in the tax burden palatable during the period from 1914 to 1980. The welfare state couldn't be funded solely by taxing the wealthiest 1 percent. But for the rest of the population to accept collectivizing a growing share of their wealth to fund education and healthcare, the middle and working classes had to have the assurance that the wealthy were paying at least as much as they. From this perspective, the increasingly progressive tax system was a decisive factor in building the welfare state, providing a contractual basis for taxation that made the rising tax levies acceptable.

Today, on the other hand, the tax system is a great source of problems. The middle and lower classes may have the impression—and it's not just an impression either—that the wealthy are largely avoiding taxes, since, despite the theoretical tax rates, there are many loopholes and strategies available to the wealthy for lowering their tax exposure.

Taxes on inheritance have followed a similar course (fig. 13). What is striking is how high the highest rate climbed in the United States, the United Kingdom, and Japan in the mid-twentieth century. This contrasts with France and Germany, for example—in part because the redistribution of wealth in those two countries was the result of war, destruction, and inflation. It's interesting to note that the only time when Germany had a high tax rate on inheritances (and also on income) was from 1945 to 1948, when that tax climbed to 90 percent. This corresponds to the period when Germany's tax policy was devised by the United States, because the

Allied Control Council had the responsibility for setting tax rates in Germany. The Americans were not especially trying to punish the German elites, since they were doing the same thing at home. The United States believed at the time that this was all part of their "civilizational package": they would introduce democratic institutions to Germany along with a tax structure that would keep the democracy from becoming plutocratic. How exotic it all sounds today! Yet it wasn't that long ago, and it's important to look back on this history, if only to realize how much our views have changed.

There remains one important point about the historic reduction in inequality during the twentieth century that I'd like to spend some time on now: the collapse of international assets, and specifically colonial assets (fig. 15). This phenomenon relates to France and the United Kingdom particularly: until 1913, these two countries were accumulating considerable assets around the world. The assets took the form of shares in the Suez Canal, railroads in Russia and Argentina, and the government debt imposed on Haiti, Morocco, China, and the Ottoman Empire, which amounted to veritable military tributes. Altogether, the French and the British owned debt worth a year of France's

FIG. 15 Foreign assets in historical perspective: The height of colonial ownership in France and Britain

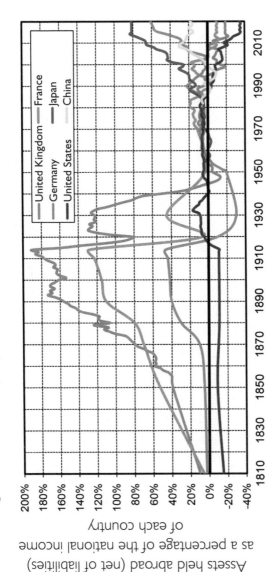

Net foreign assets—the assets held abroad by owners residing in a particular country (including those owned by the government) minus the assets held in that country by owners in the rest of the world—amounted to 191 percent of the national income in the United Kingdom in 1914 and 125 percent of the national income in France. In 2020, net foreign assets came to 82 percent of the national revenue in Japan, 61 percent in Germany, and 19 percent in China. See: piketty.pse.ens.fr/egalite national revenue and two years of the United Kingdom's. The earnings from this debt—in the form of interest, dividends, and rents—brought in 5 percent of France's national revenue and 10 percent of the United Kingdom's. For France alone, this was equivalent to the industrial production of the entire northeast section of the country, and it allowed for the financing of a persistent structural trade deficit. Between 1880 and 1914, the trade deficit rose to 2 or 3 percent, at the same time as 5 to 10 percent of the national income was arriving from the rest of the world as income and capital. These funds not only covered the trade deficit but allowed the practice of buying up the rest of the world to continue. It was equivalent to the situation where the rent you pay your landlord allows him to purchase the rest of the building.

These were highly charged and volatile situations, and they were only kept stable thanks to colonial governments and military force. The system fell apart with the outbreak of World War I. The new international circumstances were partly responsible: outright expropriations, the repudiation of Russian treasury bonds when the Bolsheviks came to power, the nationalization of the Suez Canal, et cetera. Partly responsible, too, was the cost of the war: French and British property owners were forced to sell a large share of their foreign debt to lend their governments the funds to pursue their wars—wars that were destroying the remainder of their nations' industrial capital. This slightly absurd process of self-destruction is at the heart of the history of Europe from 1914 to 1945.

WHAT TO DO WITH THE DEBT?

In terms of property interests, these pre-1914 colonial and foreign assets were turned into public debt thirty years later, in 1945. This debt came to 200 or 300 percent of national income, which is to say more than Greece's debt today—except that the debt belonged to the considerably larger economies of Germany, France, and the United Kingdom. The lesson here is that these debts were quickly disposed of, and they were never repaid. Several methods were used to make them disappear, including outright cancellation and inflation, which is not necessarily the optimum course, with Germany and Japan providing the most significant examples (fig. 16).

Germany passed through a first period of high inflation in the 1920s, which allowed it to retire the debt it had accumulated as a result of World War I. But this inflation destroyed German society and

FIG. 16 Public debt: alternating between accumulation and cancellation

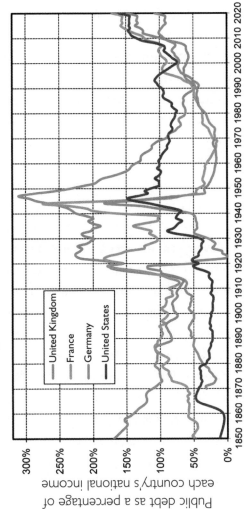

Public debt increased greatly in the wake of the two world wars, reaching 150 percent to 300 percent of national income in 1945–50 before plunging abruptly in Germany and France (cancellations of debt, special taxes on private wealth, high inflation), and more gradually in the United Kingdom and the United States. Public debt again increased sharply following the 2008 financial crisis and the 2020 epidemic. NB: not included is the debt imposed on Germany by the Treaty of Versailles (1919), amounting to more than 300 percent of the country's national income and which never even began to be repaid. See: piketty.pse.ens.fr/egalite contributed to the rise of Nazism. After World War II, the German government devised another, non-inflationary way of getting rid of its public debt: a monetary reform that divided the value of old debts by a hundred, coupled with a system of extremely high levies on the holders of large assets, so as to compensate for the losses to small and medium asset holders; the largest fortunes were assessed at up to 50 percent of their asset value. Germany adopted this reform in 1952, and it remained in force until the 1980s.

When we hear Germans speaking on the subject of economics today and saying how absolutely essential it is for Greece to repay its debt down to the last euro, these events seem very far in the past . . . It's often the way of things: history's major players have a short memory, especially when it works to their advantage. I think we should resist this historical amnesia, however. It's worth recalling that the problem of public debt has been dealt with in different ways over the course of history; there's no right way. We could look back, for instance, to the French Revolution, when the Directory simply declared bankruptcy on two-thirds of France's public debt.

The levels of public debt that we see today in the wake of COVID are not unprecedented; numerous instances of comparable debt have occurred, particularly in the history of Europe. The good news, first, is that we've always managed to deal with it. And second, there is a variety of solutions, which come with a range of adjustments and costs that can differ widely according to the case. The numbers therefore mask a social conflict. We aren't in debt to the planet Mars, it's a domestic debt, one that has to be treated politically. Looking back over history allows us to realize that these situations are not nearly as set in stone as people sometimes pretend.

I'd also like to emphasize that developing the welfare state involves more than redistributing money: it equally and above all requires taking certain goods and services out of the marketplace. The growth of certain sectors such as education, healthcare, pensions, housing, and infrastructure demonstrates that some areas of the economy can be organized to function outside of the logic of the market and capitalism. It may seem trivial, but a sector like healthcare represents 10 percent of the national income. That's a lot more than the automobile industry, for example, and it's a sector that in most countries is mainly structured around public spending. Outside of government, this sector brings together a large number of for-profit and not-for-profit actors, associations, et cetera. It may not be the best imaginable configuration, but any comparison between the United States' system—based largely on a for-profit structure—and the European system almost always shows the former to disadvantage. As we all know, the U.S. system costs more, and its public health results are disastrous when compared to Europe's.

What happens is that a system of public funding and public organizations develops around these goods and services, managed according to criteria that aren't profit-driven. Clearly, this has occurred in the education sector, for example. In Chile, however, Pinochet's regime went to great lengths to establish a for-profit educational system, but it was a great failure. There have also been joint-stock companies, such as Trump University in the United States, which have not worked at all. Private educational institutions in the United States do not generate or distribute profits. That doesn't mean they're perfect, as large donors acquire power and arrange for their children to gain admission, among other unfortunate developments. All the same, when you donate a chunk of money to Stanford or Harvard, it doesn't give you a 50 percent voting share in perpetuity. The power relations are a little different than in a joint-stock company. And in the education and healthcare sectors, no one wants to return to, or develop, a purely for-profit system. Why? Because as people have collectively realized, and as history has amply illustrated, the pursuit of profit can in many sectors destroy the intrinsic incentives that lead one to teach, provide healthcare, and perform other activities of that kind.

This important lesson applies not only to education and healthcare but also to culture and the media, where profit-seeking and the private ownership of stock create many problems. That's why many structures for nonprofits (trusts and foundations, for instance) have been developed over time—the British newspaper *The Guardian* and the French daily *France-Ouest*, for instance, are both nonprofits. None of these experiments has been perfect, but people started thinking about structures of this kind a long time ago in such diverse fields as transportation, power distribution, local administration, and water management.

In the long run, I think that this process of taking goods and services out of the marketplace should be pursued, that it should be extended to larger and larger sectors, and that it could potentially represent the near totality of a country's economic activity. It would take decentralization, as well as the participation of organizations and communities, a reliance on public funding through progressive taxation of income and wealth, and a better distribution of power in corporations and the residual for-profit sector, as I outlined earlier. Much still needs to be invented, but the important point is that it's not simply a question of redistributing money. It goes well beyond that. The trend to remove whole sectors of the economy from the marketplace is one there's no going back on.

NATURE AND INEQUALITY

I'd like to end this text with an examination of the interplay between nature, culture, and inequality in the context of the destruction of nature, the capital tied up in nature. I'm going to discuss data relating to climate change and carbon emissions; but we could focus on data of equal interest relating to other aspects of man's impact on nature. The important point I'd like to make is that the challenges posed by climate and the environment are intimately linked to inequality.

No credible solution to the challenge of global warming is imaginable without a drastic reduction in inequality and without new progress toward a greater level of equality—first, because of the substantial disparities in carbon emissions between the countries of the Global North and South, and

FIG. 17 Carbon emissions worldwide, 2010–18

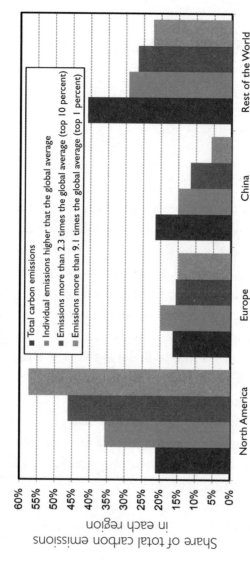

From 2010 to 2018, North America's share of total carbon emissions (direct and indirect) was 21 percent on average. The United States and Canada also accounted for 36 percent of individual emissions above the global average (which is 6.2 tons of CO_2 per year). 46 percent of emissions greater than 2.3 times the global average (that is, the top 10 percent of individual emissions worldwide, responsible for 45 percent of total emissions, as against 13 percent for the bottom 50 percent of emitters), and 57 percent of emissions greater than 9.1 times the average (that is, the top 1 percent of individual emissions worldwide, responsible for 14 percent of total emissions). See: piketty.pse.ens.fr/egalite second because of the carbon emission inequalities within countries.

The graph above (fig. 17), which focuses on disparities between countries, is based on research conducted with Lucas Chancel in our research lab on world inequality. The distribution of total carbon emissions, in the aggregate, is shown in purple: we can see that North America, Europe, and China emit carbon at roughly comparable levels. Yet their populations are very different in size and very different in their emission levels. I should point out that this data has been corrected for the emissions embedded in imports: all too often, we account only for the emissions generated domestically, ignoring emissions that are subcontracted for outside the country and are then consumed when those goods are imported. By incorporating this factor, the graph above gives a more balanced account of the situation.

But let's turn our particular attention to the other colors. The green bar, for example, represents not the country's share of total emissions but its share of very large carbon emitters, those whose individual emissions are more than nine times the global average. The global average for the seven billion humans on the planet is approximately six tons of carbon per year. The emissions shown in green therefore correspond to those emitted at a rate of more than fifty-four tons per person; they are equivalent to the top 1 percent of individual emissions. That 1 percent by itself has higher carbon emissions than the 50 percent of the planet's population who produce the least emissions. More than 55 percent of these high emissions come from North America, with Europe next highest, followed by China.

The responsibility for carbon emissions is thus distributed across the globe very asymmetrically. It's entirely imaginable that when the devastation from climate catastrophes becomes even greater than it is today, some countries will demand reparations from others and possibly revisit their trade arrangements with them. I don't know what degree of catastrophe it will take to bring us to that point, but the truth is that the current situation is highly asymmetrical.

The second aspect concerns the disparities within given countries. This graph (fig. 18), drawn from the *World Inequality Report 2022*, shows carbon emission levels in tons per person, divided into the same groups we used before in graphing income and wealth, that is, comparing the bottom 50 percent (those who emit the least carbon),

FIG. 18 Emissions per person per region across the world, 2019

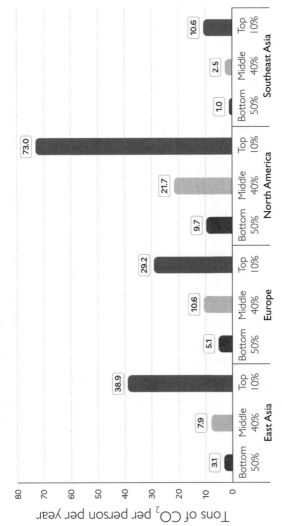

An individual carbon footprint is composed of emissions from domestic consumption, public and private investments, and the net import of goods and services from other parts of the world. These estimates are based on a combination of tax data, household studies, and import-export tables. Emissions are divided equally among household members.
See: wir2022.wid.world/methodology and Chancel (2021).

the top 10 percent, and the 40 percent in the middle. In Europe, the 50 percent who emit the least carbon—who more or less correspond to the bottom 50 percent economically—are at the five-ton level (four or four and half tons in France). To reach a sustainable level of carbon pollution, these emissions would have to fall to two or three tons. This group is therefore almost in sight of the official goals set for 2030 or 2040. By contrast, the top 10 percent are at twenty-nine tons, thirty tons, and even thirty-five tons per person. And if we were to look only at the top 1 percent in Europe, we would find them emitting at rates of sixty to seventy tons. In the United States, the top 10 percent are already emitting at a rate of more than seventy tons per person per year.

An emission-reduction policy, therefore, that proposed a fixed cut across the entire population would inevitably run into difficulties. It would be hard to convince people who are emitting four or five tons per year that they should reduce their emissions by the same proportion as people emitting thirty or even seventy tons. A strategy that increased energy costs at the same rate for everyone would never be accepted. On the contrary, such a policy would inevitably provoke, in the years and decades ahead, a tax revolt of the kind that the *gilets jaunes* (yellow vests) recently spearheaded in France. All the more so as these solutions often spare the energy consumed by the richest group—jet fuel in particular.

It's hard to see how else to meet these challenges than by asking those whose carbon emissions are highest to make reductions that are proportionally higher. This would call for putting a whole system in place that would include such tools as a progressive carbon card. It would also call for quite a drastic reduction in the income and wealth gaps.

CONCLUSION

Working from historical data, I find it difficult to predict how the present situation will develop and what form the future will take. But I'll offer two hypotheses all the same.

First, once the consequences of climate change start having a more concrete effect on the lives of individuals, it's not impossible that attitudes toward the economic system may shift very quickly, in Europe as in the rest of the world.

Second, I hope I've convinced you that the history of inequality is not a long, tranquil stream. Many battles have been fought on behalf of equality and can be fought on its behalf; many have been won. Over the long haul, there has been a general trend toward equality, a real if limited one. Questions about the economy, about finance, government debt, and wealth distribution are too important to be left in the hands of a small group of economists and experts, many of them very conservative. Instead of widening the historical and comparative perspective, they often look through the wrong end of the telescope to find narrow solutions. We need other social science researchers—historians, sociologists, political scientists, anthropologists, ethnologists— to sink their teeth into these questions, grapple with their technical aspects, and take a stand. These issues shouldn't be left to others. The democratization of economic and historical knowledge may, should, and ought to become an important part of a movement whose aim is to democratize society as a whole and better apportion power.

REFERENCES

Chancel, Lucas, Thomas Piketty, Emmanuel Saez, and Gabriel Zucman, eds. *World Inequality Report 2022*. Cambridge, Mass.: The Belknap Press of Harvard University Press, 2022.

Piketty, Thomas. *A Brief History of Equality*. Translated by Steven Rendall. Cambridge, Mass.: The Belknap Press of Harvard University Press, 2022.

———. *Capital and Ideology*. Translated by Arthur Goldhammer. Cambridge, Mass.: The Belknap Press of Harvard University Press, 2020.

World Inequality Database:
https://wid.world/

Lecture Materials:
http://piketty.pse.ens.fr/files/Piketty2022SE.pdf

CREDITS

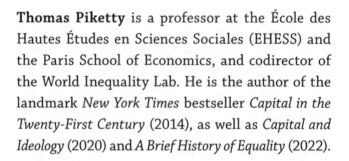

Thomas Piketty is a professor at the École des Hautes Études en Sciences Sociales (EHESS) and the Paris School of Economics, and codirector of the World Inequality Lab. He is the author of the landmark *New York Times* bestseller *Capital in the Twenty-First Century* (2014), as well as *Capital and Ideology* (2020) and *A Brief History of Equality* (2022).

Willard Wood grew up in France and has translated more than thirty works of fiction and nonfiction from the French. He has won the Lewis Galantière Award for Literary Translation and received a National Endowment for the Arts Fellowship in Translation. His recent translations include Giuliano da Empoli's *The Wizard of the Kremlin* (Other Press 2023) and Patrick Boucheron's *Trace and Aura* (Other Press 2022).